New Careers for the
21st Century:
Finding Your Role in
the Global Renewal

ENVIRONMENTAL
SCIENCE & PROTECTION:

KEEPING OUR PLANET GREEN

New Careers for the 21st Century: Finding Your Role in the Global Renewal

New Careers for the
21st Century:
Finding Your Role in
the Global Renewal

ENVIRONMENTAL
SCIENCE & PROTECTION:

KEEPING OUR PLANET GREEN

by Cordelia Strange

Mason Crest Publishers

ENVIRONMENTAL SCIENCE & PROTECTION:

KEEPING OUR PLANET GREEN

MASON CREST PUBLISHERS INC.
370 Reed Road
Broomall, Pennsylvania 19008
(866)MCP-BOOK (toll free)
www.masoncrest.com

First Printing
9 8 7 6 5 4 3 2 1

Library of Congress Cataloging-in-Publication Data

Strange, Cordelia.
  Environmental science & protection : keeping our planet green / by Cordelia Strange.
        p. cm. — (New careers for the 21st century : finding your role in America's renewal)
  Includes bibliographical references and index.
  ISBN 978-1-4222-1813-6   ISBN 978-1-4222-1811-2 (series)
  ISBN 978-1-4222-2034-4 (ppb)   ISBN 978-1-4222-2032-0 (series ppb)
  1. Environmental sciences—Vocational guidance—Juvenile literature. 2. Environmental protection—Vocational guidance—Juvenile literature.   I. Title. II. Title: Environmental science and protection.
  GE60.S77 2011
  333.72—dc22
                        2010011418

Produced by Harding House Publishing Service, Inc.
www.hardinghousepages.com
Interior design by MK Bassett-Harvey.
Cover design by Torque Advertising + Design.
Printed in USA by Bang Printing.

CONTENTS

INTRODUCTION

Be careful as you begin to plan your career.

To get yourself in the best position to begin the career of your dreams, you need to know what the "green world" will look like and what jobs will be created and what jobs will become obsolete. Just think, according to the Bureau of Labor Statistics, the following jobs are expected to severely decline by 2012:

• word processors and data-entry keyers

• stock clerks and order fillers

• secretaries

• electrical and electronic equipment assemblers

• computer operators

• telephone operators

• postal service mail sorters and processing-machine operators

• travel agents

These are just a few of the positions that will decrease or become obsolete as we move forward into the century.

You need to know what the future jobs will be. How do you find them? One way is to look where money is being invested. Many firms and corporations are now making investments in startup and research enterprises. These companies may become the "Microsoft" and "Apple" of the twenty-first century. Look at what is being researched and what technology is needed to obtain the results.

Green world, green economy, green technology—they all say the same things: the way we do business today is changing. Every industry will be shaped by the world's new focus on creating a sustainable lifestyle, one that won't deplete our natural and economic resources.

The possibilities are unlimited. Almost any area that will conserve energy and reduce the dependency on fossil fuels is open to new and exciting career paths. Many of these positions have not even been identified yet and will only come to light as the technology progresses and new discoveries are made in the way we use that technology. And the best part about this is that our government is behind us. The U.S. government wants to help you get the education and training you'll need to succeed and grow in this new and changing economy. The U.S. Department of Labor has launched a series of initiatives to support and promote green job creation. To view the report, visit: www.dol.gov/dol/green/earthday_reportA.pdf.

The time to decide on your future is now. This series, NEW CAREERS FOR THE 21ST CENTURY: FINDING YOUR ROLE IN THE GLOBAL RENEWAL, can act as the first step toward your continued education, training, and career path decisions. Take the first steps that will lead you—and the planet—to a productive and sustainable future.

Mike Puglisi
Department of Labor, District I Director (New York/New Jersey)
IAWP (International Association of Workforce Professionals)

A [hu]man is related to all nature.

—Ralph Waldo Emerson

CHAPTER **1**
INTRODUCTION TO ENVIRONMENTAL SCIENCE

WORDS TO KNOW

global warming: The average increase in temperature of the atmosphere near the earth's surface, which can contribute to changes in global climate patterns. Increasingly, the term climate change is preferred because it conveys that there are other changes occurring besides rising temperatures.

ecosystems: Places having unique physical features, encompassing air, water, and land, and including habitats that support plant and animal life.

interdisciplinary: Involving more than one academic discipline or division.

monitor: To keep track of, to watch and measure regularly.

sediments: The solid materials that settle at the bottom of a liquid.

watershed: An area of land from which all water flows to the same final place.

municipal: Having to do with a city's government.

ozone layer: An upper region of the atmosphere that contains high levels of the molecule ozone, which is composed of three oxygen atoms. The ozone layer serves to absorb solar radiation, preventing it from reaching the Earth's surface.

Industrial Revolution: The increase in machine use and factory production that began at the end of the eighteenth century.

emissions: Substances that are discharged into the air.

What will the future be like? How will our lives change? Besides fun guesses about where we will live and what vehicles we will drive, a more serious concern is what the environment will be like.

Since humans have been on the Earth, we have been changing the environment to fit our needs. Growing crops, raising livestock, constructing houses, driving cars—everything we do has an effect on the natural environment. Unfortunately many of the effects have been negative and may have lasting impacts on the planet. *Global warming*, water and air pollution, and the loss of *ecosystems* are just a few of the problems facing us today. The good news is there are actions we can take to prevent further issues, and hopefully even to correct some of the negative effects. There are even people who devote their careers to environmental issues.

CHOOSING THE RIGHT CAREER

The young adults of today will be the job force of tomorrow, so choosing a career that will best fit with the needs of the changing world will be important to job satisfaction and a successful life. With the vast array of career and job options, young adults need to understand which work will be the best match for their interests, talents, goals, and personality types. If you are interested in protecting and restoring the environment, then a career as an environmental scientist might be right for you.

Certain job industries are expected to gain importance within the early decades of the twenty-first century. The opportunities for environmental scientists are expected to increase faster than the average rate for other jobs. According to the United States Bureau of Labor Statistics, the number of jobs across all indus-

Types of Environmental Scientists and Specialists

climate change analysts
ecologists
environmental biologists
environmental chemists
environmental restoration planners
environmental science and protection technicians
industrial ecologists
soil scientists

tries is expected to increase by 11 percent through the year 2018, while the number of jobs for environmental scientists and specialists is expected to increase by 28 percent.

WHAT IS ENVIRONMENTAL SCIENCE?

Environmental science is the application of science to the study of the environment and the solution of environmental problems. Environmental science is an *interdisciplinary* field, using aspects of chemistry, biology, physics, and geology, as well as other sciences.

Environmental scientists find, study, and try to fix environmental problems such as climate change or pollution. They study what is in the air, water, and soil to make sure that the environment is healthy. When studies show that the environment is in trouble, environmental scientists suggest ways to clean the environment. Environmental science is incredibly varied because there are so many environmental issues needing investigation in today's world.

ENVIRONMENTAL ISSUES

WATER

Water is essential to life on earth. According to the United States Geological Survey (USGS), about 60 percent of the human body is water, and about 70 percent of the Earth's surface is covered by water. Because of clean water's importance to human life and to the planet in general, water pollution is of major concern to environmental scientists.

Environmental scientists test water sources in order to *monitor* water quality. This monitoring can include measurements of dissolved oxygen, *sediments*, nutrients, metals, oils, and pesticides. The scientists also check temperature, flow, color, and the health of aquatic wildlife.

Did You Know?
Every day, a person must replace about 2/3 of a gallon (or 2.4 liters) of water through drinking fluids or via absorption from food.

Scientists will monitor water in all parts of a *watershed*, in order to learn about interactions between differ-

The Chesapeake Bay watershed encompasses 64,000 m2 (166,000 km2) and includes six states, from New York down to West Virginia.

ent points in the system. Pollution entering a stream in one region can flow to the drinking water of a town miles away. Learning about these interactions can help reduce pollution and increase the safety of *municipal* water systems.

AIR AND CLIMATE CHANGE

Just like water pollution, air pollution can come from many sources, such as factories or cars. Polluted air threatens human health, as well as the health of animals, plants, and entire ecosystems. Air pollution is also one of the factors contributing to *ozone layer* damage and climate change. Environmental scientists work to improve air quality by locating and reducing sources of pollution.

Climate change is one of the major environmental issues facing the world today. Since the *Industrial Revolution*, human activity, such as the burning of fossil fuels, has resulted in *emissions* that absorb and emit heat, and reflect light. These emissions increase the amount of carbon dioxide (CO2) methane (CH4), nitrous oxide (N2O) and sulfur hexafluoride (SF6) in the atmosphere. These gases act like a greenhouse, trapping heat and increasing the temperature of the planet.

In addition to increasing temperatures, the changes in the atmosphere have likely caused changes in precipitation patterns,

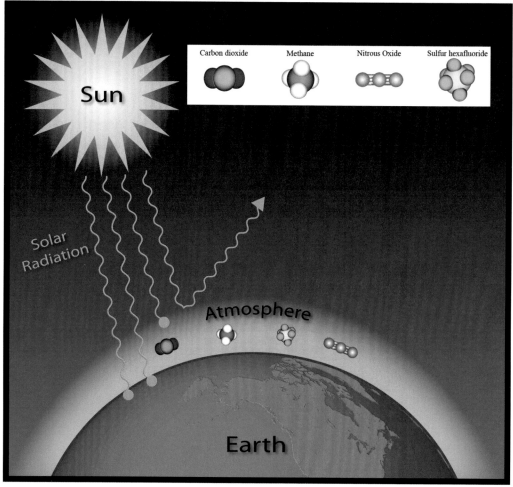

The greenhouse effect is caused by an increase in gases in the atmosphere that trap heat close to the surface of the planet.

storms, and sea level. The climate and these other features of the climate can vary naturally, so determining what is due to human activity and what is natural can be challenging.

Many environmental scientists focus specifically on the issue of climate change. These scientists study the climate of the past and the present in order to better forecast the climate of the future. Predicting the future changes includes climate modeling to plan for likely impacts on ecosystems and human health. Many of these environmental scientists are also active in the development of new ways to slow or stop climate change and its effects.

WASTES AND POLLUTION

People create a lot of waste—garbage from our towns and homes (municipal solid waste), hazardous waste from our industry, nearly everything we do leaves behind some kind of waste. Waste that enters the environment pollutes ecosystems and can affect both human and animal health. Environmental scientists study this pollution, help to discover the sources of potential contamination, and work with towns, businesses, and industries to create regulations and prevent further environmental pollution.

Did You Know?
According the EPA. in 2008 each person created an average of 4.5 pounds of waste each day!

HUMAN HEALTH

Protecting human health is a vital reason for an environmental scientist's job. All the aforementioned issues can negatively impact human health. By finding the sources of pollution and developing new ways to prevent it, environmental scientists are creating

Total MSW Generation (by material), 2008
250 Million Tons (before recycling)

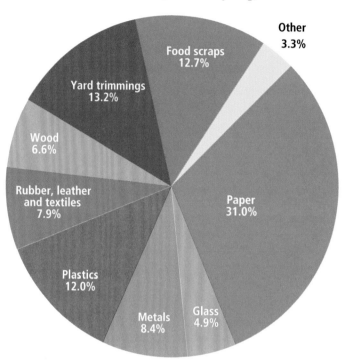

People produce a lot of solid waste each year. This chart shows the types of municipal solid waste, or MSW, produced in the United States in 2008.

a healthier future for all people. Research includes studies on how air pollution affects children and people with asthma and how water contaminants may affect beachgoers. Environmental scientists work with state and local agencies, as well as volunteer and other citizens groups, to monitor air and water quality and to reduce human exposure to contaminants in the air, land, and water.

Interested in the Past?

Perhaps a career as a paleoclimatologist would be right for you. Just be prepared for some possibly cold work environments!

Paleoclimatology is the study of past climate changes. The more we understand about climate changes in the past, the better equipped we will be for the changes occurring in the world today. Paleoclimatologists can learn about past climate from tree rings, ice cores, corals, and ancient lake and ocean sediments.

Ice cores offer one of the most valuable sources of climate information on the planet. Drilling projects operate in places where ice sheets stretch back thousands of years to gather the most complete records about climate change in the past, as well as levels of gases like methane and CO_2.

The Greenland Ice Sheet Project was a decade-long ice core project to drill into the Greenland ice sheet from surface to bedrock. On Thursday, July 1, 1993, this goal was accomplished, when the team bored nearly two miles down to the bedrock. The resulting environmental records obtained from the ice cores span over 200,000 years of the Earth's history. Pictured here, the ice cores show the sharp change from clear to silty ice that occurs at a depth of 1.889 miles (3040.33 m). The transition is followed by alternating bands of silty and clear ice followed by progressively siltier ice until contact with bedrock.

ECOSYSTEMS

Protecting human health is important to environmental scientists, but so is protecting the health of ecosystems. Ecosystems offer many important services to the planet and to human health. Depending on the type of ecosystem, benefits include clean air and water, fertile soil, pollination, and flood control. Environmental scientists perform studies aimed at understanding all the services ecosystems provide to humans. Environmental scientists also conduct research that addresses all the factors, both natural and human, affecting ecosystems. Finally, these scientists use this research to aid in environmental management decisions and to halt processes that are causing damage to the world's important ecosystems.

This image shows an example of a large-scale ecosystem. Pollution causing problems in one part of the system will lead to issues everywhere else.

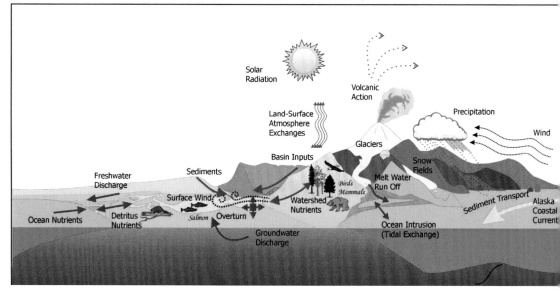

What Kind of Person Are You?

Career-counseling experts know that certain kinds of people do best in certain kinds of jobs. John L. Holland developed the following list of personality types and the kinds of jobs that are the best match for each type. See which one (or two) are most like you. The more you understand yourself, the better you'll be able to make a good career plan for yourself.

- **Realistic personality:** This kind of person likes to do practical, hands-on work. He or she will most enjoy working with materials that can be touched and manipulated, such as wood, steel, tools, and machinery. This personality type enjoys jobs that require working outdoors, but he or she does NOT enjoy jobs that require a lot of paperwork or close teamwork with others.

- **Investigative personality:** This personality type likes to work with ideas. He or she will enjoy jobs that require lots of thinking and researching. Jobs that require mental problem solving will be a good fit for this personality.

- **Artistic personality:** This type of person enjoys working with forms, designs, and patterns. She or he likes jobs that require self-expression—and that don't require following a definite set of rules.

- **Social personality:** Jobs that require lots of teamwork with others, as well as teaching others, are a good match for this personality type. These jobs often involve helping others in some way.

- **Enterprising personality:** This person will enjoy planning and starting new projects, even if that involves a degree of risk-taking. He or she is good at making decisions and leading others.

- **Conventional personality:** An individual with this type of personality likes to follow a clear set of procedures or routines. He or she doesn't want to be the boss but prefers to work under someone else's leadership. Jobs that require working with details and facts (more than ideas) are a good fit for this personality.

A life's work is born out of your visions, values, and ideals. It's giving life to your values, anchoring them in the everyday world of action.

—Laurence G. Boldt

CHAPTER 2
ENVIRONMENTAL SCIENTISTS

WORDS TO KNOW

degradation: The wearing away, or erosion, of land by water, wind, ice, or other process.

conservation: The careful use of natural resources to prevent waste or loss.

replenishment: The process of filling up something that has been used up.

risk assessment: A report that shows where an organization is most likely to suffer a loss and the estimated cost of recovery in the event of damage.

consulting firms: Businesses that charge money to provide professional advice to other businesses or organizations.

policy: A course of action followed by a government.

geologic: Related to the study of the origin, history, and physical structure of the Earth.

mathematical modeling: A mathematical representation of reality that attempts to explain behavior and tries to find a solution to a problem.

systems analysis: The study of an activity or procedure to determine the desired end and the most efficient method of obtaining this end.

thermodynamics: The branch of physics concerned with the conversion of heat into different forms of energy.

restoration: The process of getting something back to what it was originally.

As student or young adult interested in an environmental science career, you have many choices from which to pick for your career path. Knowing what interests you most ahead of time will help you make the right choices regarding education and training. Take a look at the boxed material on personality types at the end of each chapter in this book.

The first step to choosing a career in environmental science is understanding what environmental scientists do and what specializations exist within the field.

ENVIRONMENTAL PROTECTION

Environmental scientists use their knowledge of chemistry, biology, or other sciences to protect the environment by identifying problems and finding solutions that reduce risks to the health of the environment and to humans. They observe and analyze air, food, water, and soil to determine ways to clean and preserve the environment. Understanding issues involved in protecting the environment is central to the work of environmental scientists.

RESEARCH

Environmental science research includes work in both the lab and in the field to monitor resources and determine contaminants and sources of pollution. Research often involves the collection of samples for testing. Environmental science and protection technicians—workers who are supervised by environmental scientists—perform much of the work of collecting and testing samples.

This environmental scientist is taking samples of spring water to test for chemicals and other contaminants.

ENVIRONMENTAL REGULATIONS

Environmental scientists use their understanding of environmental issues like *degradation*, *conservation*, recycling, or *replenishment* to design and monitor waste disposal sites, preserve water supplies, reclaim contaminated land, write *risk assessments*,

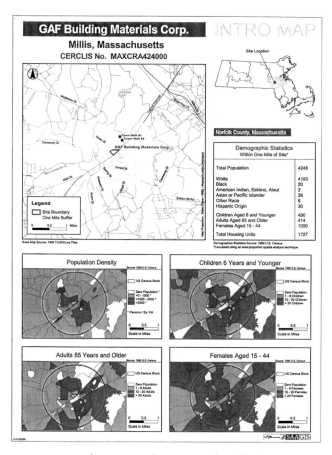

This report was prepared to assess the potential public health impact of possible contaminants released into the surrounding community by the GAF Building Materials Corporation in Millis, Massachusetts.

make new laws about protecting the environment, or help companies abide by existing laws.

Federal, state, and local governments create environmental regulations that are meant to guarantee clean air, safe drinking water, and uncontaminated soil. These regulations limit construction or restrict levels of pollution. Many environmental scientists work for the government to ensure the regulations are followed in order to limit the impact of human activity on the environment. Other government-employed environmental scientists monitor pollution and its effects on population health. Private companies, such as *consulting firms*, also employ environmental scientists for help complying with regulations and laws.

Policy Formation

Environmental scientists who work on *policy* formation try to identify ways to modify human behavior to avoid problems such as ground-water contamination and depletion of the ozone layer. Environmental scientists who work in policy formation or in managerial positions have usually first spent time performing research or learning about environmental laws and regulations.

Specializations in Environmental Science

Environmental scientists do work and have training similar to other physical or life scientists, but they focus on environmental issues. Many specialize in subfields such as environmental ecology and conservation, environmental chemistry, environmental biology, or fisheries science. These specialties affect the specific activities that environmental scientists perform.

Environmental Science Technicians

Science technicians are the laborers of the environmental science industry. They assist scientists in research and development and

Science technicians perform laboratory tasks under the supervision of more skilled scientists.

help to invent and improve products and processes. Their jobs are more practically oriented than those of scientists. In other words, scientists develop ideas, and the technicians do the work that tests or develops those ideas into real-world applications.

Most science technicians specialize in a particular field, learning their skills and working in the same disciplines in which scientists work. Environmental science and protection technicians, therefore, are those technicians that work with environmental scientists to monitor environmental resources and determine the contaminants and sources of pollution in the environment.

GEOSCIENTISTS AND HYDROLOGISTS

Geoscientists and hydrologists study the composition, structure, and other physical aspects of the Earth's *geologic* past and present by analyzing the composition of earth, rock, and water. Many geoscientists and hydrologists help to search for natural resources such as groundwater, minerals, metals, and petroleum. Others work closely with other environmental scientists to preserve and clean up the environment. Geoscientists usually study and work in a specific field, such as geology, geophysics, or hydrology.

Did You Know?

Since the mid 1970s, the average surface temperature of the Earth has warmed about 1°F. That may not seem like much, but even small changes like this can have drastic changes on the Earth's ecosystems and climate patterns.

CLIMATE CHANGE ANALYSTS

Climate change analysts research and analyze policy developments related to climate change. They also make climate-related recommendations for awareness, legislation, or fundraising campaigns.

ENVIRONMENTAL ECOLOGISTS

Environmental ecologists study the relationships between organisms and their environments and the effects of factors such as

Real Life Environmental Scientist

Making the World Safe for Boy Scouts and Four-Wheelers

Chris Rohrer is a senior reclamation specialist with the Utah Division of Oil, Gas and Mining. He manages projects to close dangerous abandoned mines from public access. He states, "During the summer field season I spend time outdoors investigating abandoned mine operations for reclamation potential and conducting site-specific research on mine hazards and safety and environmental conditions."

For a job like Chris's, interdisciplinary training is valuable, as the solutions to environmental problems require many different perspectives. A strong core of natural science knowledge is necessary, but should be complemented by a well-rounded, liberal arts curriculum, because environmental problems require "big-picture" solutions that cross disciplines. It is essential to be able to communicate with other specialties, as well as the general public. At various times in his career Chris has been a biologist, historian, chemist, civil engineer, accountant, administrator, artist, demographer, publicist, cartographer, ditch digger, mathematician, graphic designer, surveyor, writer, and more without ever changing jobs. This interdisciplinary nature of the work helps keep it interesting.

"I thrive on the many facets of the work," says Chris, ". . .and the varied challenges, such as trying to figure out how to safeguard a shaft while preserving the historic headframe above it and protecting bat habitat inside. There is a tangible sense of accomplishment in that."

(From naturalresources.utah.gov/employment/love-their-jobs environmental-scientist.html) population size, pollutants, rainfall, and temperature on both. They may collect, study, and report data on air, soil, and water using their knowledge of various scientific disciplines.

ECOLOGICAL MODELERS

Ecological modelers study ecosystems, pollution control, and resource management using *mathematical modeling*, *systems analysis*, *thermodynamics*, and computer techniques.

ENVIRONMENTAL CHEMISTS

Environmental chemists study various chemicals and how those chemicals affect the environment, including plants, animals, and people.

ENVIRONMENTAL RESTORATION PLANNERS

Environmental restoration planners work with field and biology staff to conduct site assessments, create management plans, supervise *restoration* projects, and develop new products. They also process, and analyze complex scientific data to develop practical strategies for environmental restoration, monitoring, or management.

WHERE DO ENVIRONMENTAL SCIENTISTS WORK?

Entry-level environmental scientists and specialists spend a significant amount of time in the field, while more experienced workers generally devote more time to office or laboratory work. Some environmental scientists, such as environmental ecologists

Environmental science technicians may work in the field, as in the case of these technicians who are collecting samples of oil from a spill.

and environmental chemists, often take field trips that involve physical activity. Environmental scientists in the field may work in warm or cold climates, in all kinds of weather. Travel often is required to meet with prospective clients.

If You Have an Investigative Personality . . .

Being an environmental scientist could be an excellent career choice for you, since it will give you lots of opportunities for research and problem-solving.

Here are some of the best jobs for you in the field of environmental science. (These tables also include the average salary you can expect to earn in U.S. dollars in these jobs and how many openings are projected to exist in the United States each year for these jobs. When you look at the average salary, remember that some positions will pay more than that and some less. The information comes from the U.S. Bureau of Labor Statistics.)

JOB	ANNUAL EARNINGS	ANNUAL OPENINGS
environmental engineer	$72,350	5,000
environmental scientist, including health	$58,380	6,960
geoscientist	$75,800	2,470
hydrologist	$68,140	687

Questions are the creative acts of intelligence.

—Frank Kingdon-Ward

ABOUT THE QUOTE

A good way to choose a career direction might be to think about the things that make you feel curious. What would you like to learn more about? What makes you feel curious and full of wonder? This feeling may be an arrow pointing you toward a life's career.

CHAPTER 3
EDUCATION AND TRAINING

WORDS TO KNOW

associate degree: The degree given to a student who completes two years of study, usually given by community colleges.

PhD: Doctor of philosophy, the degree awarded to a student beyond a master's degree, after the completion of at least three years of graduate study plus a dissertation; also known as a doctorate.

bachelor's degree: The degree given to a student who completes four years of undergraduate studies; also known as a baccalaureate degree.

private sector: The part of a nation's economy that is not controlled by the government.

vocational: Having to do with education that is focused on a certain occupation and its skills.

master's degree: The degree awarded to a student who had completed at least one year of graduate study.

remote sensing: Remote sensing is an imaging technique used to collect data about the Earth without taking a physical sample of the Earth's surface. A sensor, mounted on a satellite or other aircraft, is used to measure energy reflected from the Earth.

There is a wide range of specializations in environmental science. Depending on the chosen specialization, training and education requirements can range from an *associate degree* to a *PhD*.

A *bachelor's degree* is sufficient for most jobs in government and *private sector* companies, although a *master's degree* is often preferred. A PhD is usually only necessary for jobs in college teaching or research.

EDUCATION REQUIREMENTS

ENVIRONMENTAL SCIENCE TECHNICIANS

To qualify for a job as a science technician, applicants should have a high school degree and at least two years of specialized training or an associate degree in applied science or science-related technology. Some science technicians have a bachelor's degree in the natural sciences, while others have no formal college education and learn their skills on the job. Positions in

Interning with an environmental science technician can give a student the opportunity to get hands-on experience in different aspects of her field of interest. This Hunter College intern is working with a biological technician to collect water quality data in the ponds at the Jamaica Bay Wildlife Refuge in the Jamaica Bay Unit of Gateway National Recreation Area.

which the technician is expected to have special knowledge of one particular field require higher education. For example, biological technicians often need a bachelor's degree in biology or a closely related field.

TECHNICAL SCHOOLS

Depending on the occupation, there may be technical or *vocational* schools that train students to be scientific technicians. Many technical schools offer programs in specific disciplines. The length of these programs varies, although one-year certificate programs and two-year associate degree programs are common. Some schools offer cooperative-education or internship programs, allowing students the opportunity to work at a local company or some other workplace while attending classes during alternate terms. Participation in such programs can significantly improve a student's chance of getting a job after graduation. Many associate degree programs are designed to provide easy transfer to bachelor's degree programs at colleges or universities if the student chooses to continue his or her education.

COMMUNITY COLLEGES

Community colleges offer another option for students interested in a career in environmental science. Community colleges usually offer less technician training than a technical school, but provide more theory and general education.

Community colleges are good places to learn job skills for a number of reasons. They have low tuition and an open-admissions policy, and they offer many courses, including classes that will help prepare students for their chosen industry. Community colleges are also flexible; at most community colleges, nearly 50

Internship Opportunities

Internships are an excellent way for students to gain knowledge and experience in a given field. In addition, internships can help the student decide if that career is the right choice. A student may set out with plans to become an ecologist, for example, only to discover from real-life exposure to the work world that he or she would be better suited to a career centered around law and policy formation. Many federal, state, and local government agencies offer student internship or employment programs throughout the year. Private companies, consulting firms, or university research facilities will also often offer internships. Most government agencies and private companies offer opportunities to students at all levels of education—from the high school student to the post doctoral researcher.

High school students or college students can participate in the federal Student Temporary Employment Program (STEP) program, which offers temporary employment that will enable a student to earn money while continuing studies. The length of these positions can range from three months during the summer to longer. To qualify, you must be a U.S. citizen, be at least 16 years old, and be enrolled as a degree-seeking student. More specifically, you must be taking at least a half-time academic or vocational and technical course load at one of the following:

• accredited high school,

• technical or *vocational* school, or

• a two- or four-year accredited college or university at the undergraduate, graduate, or professional school level.

The EPA Environmental Careers Program, ECP, previously named EPA Intern Program, is a comprehensive, entry-level, professional, full-time, career development program. It involves an intensive two-year assignment to help graduates with bachelor's degrees or higher jump-start their careers and develop their potential for future advancement within the EPA. The ECP seeks graduates in a variety of academic disciplines, including physical and life sciences, business, finance, computer sciences, and policy and public administration.

More information can be found online at www.epa.gov/ohr/eip.html.

percent of the students work full time, so they offer courses at convenient times.

HANDS-ON EXPERIENCE

No matter the chosen education path, science technicians usually need hands-on training, which they can receive either in school, through an internship, or on the job. Job candidates with extensive experience using a variety of laboratory equipment, including computers and related equipment, usually require only a short period of on-the-job training. Those with a high school diploma and no college degree typically have a longer training program in which they work under the direct supervision of a more experienced technician.

ENVIRONMENTAL SCIENTISTS

A bachelor's degree in an earth science is required for most entry-level environmental scientist positions, although many companies prefer a master's degree in environmental science or a related science. Some environmental scientists and specialists have degrees in environmental science, but many earn degrees in biology, chemistry, physics, or the geosciences and then apply their education to the environment. Many jobs also require new hires to have research or work experience related to environmental science.

An advantage to earning a bachelor's degree in environmental science is that it offers general knowledge of all the natural sciences, with an emphasis on biology, chemistry, and geology. Students interested in environmental regulations should take courses in hydrology, hazardous-waste management, environmental legislation, chemistry, and geologic logging, which is the gathering of geologic data. An understanding of environmental regulations and government permit issues is also valuable.

Courses in business, finance, marketing, or economics may be useful for students interested in consulting positions. Combining environmental science with other disciplines such as business will qualify a student for a larger number of positions.

GEOSCIENTISTS AND OTHER SPECIALISTS

Some entry-level positions only require a bachelor's degree, but most geoscientists and hydrologists need a master's degree, which is the preferred educational requirement for most research positions

Real life Environmental Scientist

Limnologist

Carla Cáceres turned her childhood love of water into a career in limnology. Limnologists are scientists who study the characteristics of freshwater systems such as lakes, rivers, streams, ponds, and wetlands. They also study non-oceanic saltwater, such as the Great Salt Lake.

The job title limnologist applies to workers in many occupations who are trained in different scientific fields. A limnologist's area of specialization usually determines his or her specific occupational title. Environmental scientists, ecologists, fisheries biologists, natural resources specialists, and biogeochemists—all can be limnologists. What they share is a common focus on inland water systems. And when they work together on projects, each contributes his or her specialized knowledge.

Carla, for example, is an ecologist who studies several species of zooplankton in lakes and ponds in Michigan and Illinois. She works with scientists from the Illinois Natural History Survey, a research organization that monitors lake conditions. Limnologists' goals often relate to maintaining natural ecosystems or to understanding the potential impact of an activity, such as building houses in a wetland area.

"It's easier to manage a system if you understand it," says Carla.

in private industry, federal agencies, and state geological surveys. A PhD is necessary for high-level research and college teaching positions, but is generally not required for other jobs.

Many colleges and universities offer bachelor's and graduate degrees in the geosciences. Students who study other sciences may also qualify for some geoscience positions if their course work includes geology. Most universities do not offer degrees in hydrology, but instead offer concentrations in hydrology or water studies in their geoscience, environmental science, or engineering departments.

Licensure and Certification

Many states require geoscientists and hydrologists who offer their services directly to the public to obtain a license from a state licensing board. Licensing requirements vary but usually include education and experience requirements, and a passing score on an examination. In states that do not require a license, workers can obtain voluntary certifications. For example, the American Institute of Hydrology offers certification programs in professional hydrology that have similar requirements to state licensure programs.

Other Skills

The most successful environmental scientists have extensive computer skills. Students with experience in computer modeling, data analysis and integration, digital mapping, and *remote sensing*, will be the most prepared to enter the job market.

Communication skills are important in nearly every profession. Environmental scientists usually work as part of a team with other scientists, engineers, and technicians, and they must often write technical reports and research proposals that clearly communicate their research results or ideas to company managers, regulators, and the public. As a result, strong oral and written communication skills are essential.

Advancement

As in most careers, environmental scientists do not generally start as supervisors or managers. Technicians begin as trainees under the supervision of a scientist or more experienced technician. As they gain experience, technicians will be granted more responsibility and may eventually become supervisors.

Environmental scientists usually begin as field analysts, research assistants, or technicians in laboratories or offices. They are given more difficult assignments as they gain experience. Eventually, they may be promoted to project leader, program manager, or some other management or research position.

If You Have a Realistic Personality . . .

You might most enjoy a job as a science technician. These positions are more hands-on, more involved with the practical, physical details of environmental science, and there's a good likelihood you would spend much of your time outdoors. Technicians in some areas of environmental science make more than others. For instance, the average annual salary for geological and petroleum technicians is $50,950; there are 1,895 openings each year for these jobs. Environmental protection and health technicians have an average salary of $39,370, and there are about 8,400 job openings each year.

Technology is destructive only in the hands of people who do not realize that they are one and the same process as the universe.

—Alan Watts

ABOUT THE QUOTE

Technology has gotten a bad name. We talk about "getting back to nature," as though if we could all do so we would solve all the Earth's problems. But the reality is that we need technology to solve the problems we have created (such as climate change and pollution). If you choose a career in environmental science, you will be using technology in harmony with nature.

CHAPTER 4
JOB OPPORTUNITIES AND RELATED OCCUPATIONS

WORDS TO KNOW

fundamental: A primary principle or process upon which others are based.

zoology: The branch of biology that studies animals.

forest economics: The study of the production, consumption, and management of natural resources available in forests.

research and development: Also known as R&D, this is the work aimed at the development of new or improved concepts, products, and processes.

Once a student has chosen his or her career path and has completed the appropriate education, the next step is getting a job. But where are the most jobs available?

According the Bureau of Labor Statistics, environmental scientists and specialists held about 85,900 jobs in 2008. Around 37 percent of environmental scientists were employed in state and local governments; 21 percent in management, scientific, and technical consulting services; 15 percent in architectural, engineering, and related services; and 7 percent in the federal government, primarily in the United States Department of Agriculture (USDA), the Environmental Protection Agency (EPA), and the Department of Defense.

Science technicians held about 270,800 jobs in 2008. Biological technicians and chemical technicians filled more than half these jobs. Environmental science technicians held an

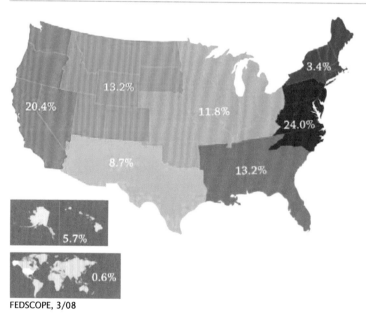

ENVIRONMENTAL SCIENCE POSITIONS
IN THE FEDERAL GOVERNMENT BY REGION

FEDSCOPE, 3/08

There are many environmental science positions available through the federal government. This map shows the regions of the country with the highest percentage of government positions.

additional 35,000 positions, most of which were for professional, scientific, and technical services firms, or for state and local governments.

EMPLOYMENT OF SCIENCE TECHNICIANS IN 2008

biological technicians	79,500
chemical technicians	66,100
environmental science and protection technicians, including health	35,000
forest and conservation technicians	34,000
agricultural and food science technicians	21,900
geological and petroleum technicians	15,200
forensic science technicians	12,800
nuclear technicians	6,400

Did You Know?

Federal, state, and local governments employ 44 percent of all environmental scientists and specialists.

Geoscientists held about 33,600 jobs in 2008, while another 8,100 were employed as hydrologists. Around 23 percent of geoscientists were employed in architectural, engineering and related services, and 19 percent worked for oil and gas extraction companies. State agencies employed another 9 percent of geoscientists. Eight percent worked for the federal government, mostly USGS and within the Department of Defense.

Related Occupations

Environmental scientists work with a wide range of other special-ists. In addition, many related occupations work on environmen-tal issues and contribute to environmental research. If you are interested in environmental preservation, you should consider these disciplines as well.

Atmospheric Scientists

Atmospheric scientists study the atmosphere and how the pro-cesses occurring in the atmosphere affect the rest of our envi-ronment. The best-known application of atmospheric science is the weather forecasting done by meteorologists. In addition to predicting the weather, atmospheric scientists attempt to iden-tify and interpret climate trends, understand past weather, and

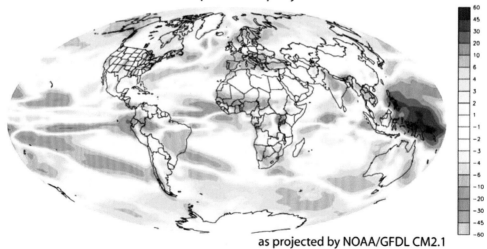

CHANGE IN PRECIPITATION BY END OF 21st CENTURY
inches of liquid water per year

as projected by NOAA/GFDL CM2.1

Atmospheric scientists use models and historical data to predict future cli-mate and weather trends. This map represents the predicted global change in precipitation by the end of the 21st century.

analyze current weather. Weather information and atmospheric research are also applied in air pollution control, agriculture, forestry, air and sea transportation, defense, and the study of possible trends in the Earth's climate, such as global warming, droughts, and ozone depletion.

Did You Know?
Climate change is expected to alter weather patterns during the twenty-first century so that wet areas get wetter and dry areas become drier.

Environmental problems have widened the scope of the meteorological profession. Environmental meteorologists study problems such as pollution and shortages of fresh water. They evaluate and report on air quality for environmental impact statements, and examine ways to control or diminish air pollution.

BIOLOGICAL SCIENTISTS

Biological scientists study living organisms and their relationship to the environment. They perform research to gain a better understanding of *fundamental* life processes. Most biological scientists specialize in one area of biology, such as *zoology* or ecology.

The research of biological scientists advances our knowledge of living organisms so that we can develop solutions to human health problems and improve the natural environment. These biological scientists mostly work in government, university, or private industry laboratories.

CHEMISTS AND MATERIALS SCIENTISTS

Everything in the environment, whether naturally occurring or of human design, is composed of chemicals. Chemists and materials scientists search for new knowledge about chemicals and use it to improve life. Chemical research has led to the discovery and development of thousands of commonly used products. Chemists and materials scientists also develop processes such as improved oil refining and petrochemical processing that save energy and reduce pollution. An environmental application of materials science is the development of better, more efficient fuel cells. Research on the chemistry of living things spurs advances in medicine, agriculture, and food processing, as well as environmental science.

CONSERVATION SCIENTISTS

Conservation scientists and foresters manage the use and development of forests, rangelands, and other natural resources. These lands supply wood products, livestock forage, minerals, and water. They serve as sites for recreational activities and provide habitats for wildlife. Some workers advise private landowners on the use and management of their land and design programs that make the land healthier and more productive. Others work to conserve or restore public or private lands. Conservation scientists and foresters often specialize in one of several areas, such as soil conservation, urban forestry, pest management, native species, or *forest economics.*

Did You Know?
Climate change is expected to increase the amount of insect-borne disease around the world. According to the Intergovernmental Panel on Climate Change (IPCC), the global population at risk from malaria will increase by between 220 million and 400 million in the next century.

Engineering Technicians

Engineering technicians use the principles and theories of science, engineering, and mathematics to solve technical problems in *research and development*, manufacturing, sales, construction, inspection, and maintenance. Their work is more narrowly focused and application oriented than that of other scientists and engineers. Many engineering technicians assist engineers and scientists, especially in research and development.

Environmental engineering tech-nicians work closely with environmental engineers and scientists in developing methods and devices used in the prevention, control, or remediation of environmental hazards. They inspect and maintain equipment related to air pollution and recycling. Some inspect water and wastewater treatment systems to ensure that pollution control requirements are met.

Engineers

Engineers apply the principles of science and mathematics to develop economical solutions to technical problems. Their work brings scientific discoveries into practical use in the real world.

Environmental engineers use the principles of biology and chemistry to develop practical solutions to environmental problems. They are involved in water and air pollution control, recycling, waste disposal, and public health issues. Environmental engineers conduct hazardous-waste management studies in which they evaluate the significance of the hazard, advise on its treatment and containment, and develop regulations to prevent mishaps. They design municipal water supply and industrial wastewater treatment systems, conduct research on the environmental impact of proposed construction projects, analyze scientific data, and perform quality-control checks.

Environmental engineers are concerned with both local and global environmental issues. Some may study and attempt to minimize the effects of acid rain, global warming, automobile emissions, and ozone depletion. They also may be involved in the protection of wildlife. Many environmental engineers work as consultants, helping their clients to comply with regulations, prevent environmental damage, and clean up hazardous sites.

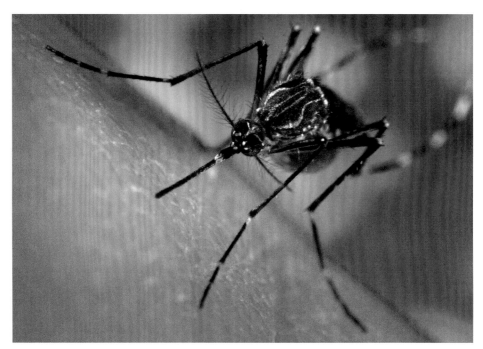

An increase in mosquitoes and the infectious diseases they carry, such as malaria, is one of the predicted effects of climate change. Epidemiologists study diseases such as malaria in order to learn how better to control the causes and how to prevent and treat the diseases.

EPIDEMIOLOGISTS

Epidemiologists investigate and describe the causes and spread of disease, and develop the means for prevention or control. Applied epidemiologists, who usually work for state health agencies, respond to disease outbreaks, determining their causes and helping to contain them. Research epidemiologists study diseases in laboratories and in the field to determine how to prevent future outbreaks. Learning how to prevent future outbreaks will be especially important in light of the predicted effects of climate change on human health.

If You Have a Social Personality . . .

Environmental scientist may not be the right career choice for you. Although scientists often are part of team, much of their work is done alone, with little interaction with others.

If You Have an Enterprising Personality . . .

You may enjoy working in a supervisory position in the field of environmental science. Keep in mind, though, that no matter how much education you have, these are usually not entry-level positions. You will have to be willing to put in your time at lower levels in order to gain the experience you need to advance to a leadership role. Once you get there, you can expect to earn considerably more, though there will likely be fewer available job openings to choose from.

Keep away from people who try to belittle your ambitions. Small people always do that, but the really great make you feel that you, too, can become great.

—Mark Twain

CHAPTER 5
THE FUTURE OF
ENVIRONMENTAL SCIENCE

The future of environmental science is bright largely because the future of the environment is in jeopardy. The environmental challenges facing the world today—climate change, pollution, and depletion of natural resources—need to be addressed before the environment has been damaged beyond repair. Environmental scientists are leaders in the movement to find new ways to live so that we can reduce the negative impact we make on the Earth, and improve the quality of life for future generations. As a result, job prospects are expected to be excellent for individuals interested in a career in environmental science or a related environmental field.

Occupational Title	SOC Code	Employment, 2008	Projected Employment, 2018	Change, 2008-18	
				Number	Percent
Environmental scientists and specialists, including health	19-2041	85,900	109,800	23,900	28

ENVIRONMENTAL SCIENTISTS

Employment is expected to grow much faster than the average for all occupations. Employment of environmental scientists and specialists is likely to increase by 28 percent between 2008 and 2018, much faster than the average 11 percent for all occupations. Job growth should be highest in private consulting firms, but job prospects are also expected to be favorable in state and local government.

Did You Know?
In October 1999, the world population reached 6 billion people, nearly doubling in size in less than 40 years!

This growth in employment will be driven by the increasing demands placed on the environment by population growth and increasing awareness of the problems caused by environmental degradation. There will also be a continued need to monitor the quality of the environment, to interpret the impact of human actions on land and water ecosystems, and to develop strategies for restoring damaged ecosystems. In addition, environmental scientists will be needed to help planners develop and construct buildings, *transportation corridors*, and utilities that protect water resources and reflect efficient and beneficial land use. Finally, demand will increase for individuals who understand policy and environmental law, since there will be an increased need to comply with complex environmental laws and regulations.

Consulting Firms

An increase in the number of environmental regulations will increase the job opportunities for environmental scientists in the consulting industry. Besides aiding in regulation compliance, many environmental scientists and specialists will find consulting work helping businesses and governments perform research and develop plans for solutions related to underground tanks, land disposal areas, and other hazardous-waste-management facilities.

New regulations will require businesses to incorporate environmental activities during all steps of the business process, which will result in a greater focus on waste minimization, resource recovery, pollution prevention, and the consideration of environmental effects during product development. This shift in focus to prevention will provide many new opportunities for environmental scientists in consulting roles.

Science Technicians

Overall, employment of science technicians is expected to grow as fast as average for the next decade. However, employment of environmental science and protection technicians is projected to grow much faster than average, at 29 percent. This is again due to the projected increase in environmental issues and the need for more workers to help regulate waste products, collect air, water, and soil samples, monitor regulation compliance, and clean up contaminated sites. Most employment opportunities are expected to be in firms that assist other companies in environmental monitoring, management, and regulatory compliance.

Occupational Title	SOC Code	Employment, 2008	Projected Employment, 2018	Change, 2008-18	
				Number	Percent
Science technicians	—	270,800	302,600	31,800	12
Agricultural and food science technicians	19-4011	21,900	23,800	1,900	9
Biological technicians	19-4021	79,500	93,500	14,000	18
Chemical technicians	19-4031	66,100	65,500	-500	-1
Geological and petroleum technicians	19-4041	15,200	15,400	200	2
Nuclear technicians	19-4051	6,400	7,000	600	9
Environmental science and protection technicians, including health	19-4091	35,000	45,200	10,100	29
Forensic science technicians	19-4092	12,800	15,300	2,500	20
Forest and conservation technicians	19-4093	34,000	36,900	2,900	9

GEOSCIENTISTS

Employment of geoscientists and hydrologists is also expected to grow faster than average over the next decade. Graduates with a master's degree in geoscience will have better job opportunities than PhDs, who will face more competition for research and college teaching jobs. Job opportunities within the geosciences will be low for graduates with only bachelor's degrees, but these graduates may have excellent opportunities in related occupations, such as high school science teachers or science technicians.

Overall, job opportunities are expected to increase by 18 percent for geoscientists and hydrologists between 2008 and 2018. The increased need for energy, environmental protection, and responsible land and water management will increase demand. Some of the increase in demand will also result from the need for more geoscience consultants to aid governments and private companies in the development of environmental management plans.

Geoscientists and hydrologists who monitor environmental pollution will also have greater job opportunities because of the continued concerns about air pollution, soil and water contamination, and the effects of pollutants on human health. In addition, geoscientists will be needed for research and consulting on many other growing environmental issues, such as land erosion, deterioration of coastal ecosystems, and climate change.

As more people move into environmentally sensitive areas, there will be an increased demand for hydrologists. In coastal regions, for example, hydrologists will be needed to assess the safety of building sites and plan for natural disasters, such as floods, or hurricanes.

Occupational Title	SOC Code	Employment, 2008	Projected Employment, 2018	Change, 2008-18	
				Number	Percent
Geoscientists and hydrologists	—	41,700	49,100	7,400	18
Geoscientists, except hydrologists and geographers	19-2042	33,600	39,400	5,900	18
Hydrologists	19-2043	8,100	9,600	1,500	18

Hydrologists also will be needed to study hazardous-waste sites and determine the effect of pollutants on soil and ground water so that engineers can design *remediation* systems. Increased government regulations, such as those regarding the management of storm water, and issues related to water conservation, deteriorating coastal environments, and rising sea levels will also stimulate employment growth for hydrologists. The best opportunities will be available for hydrologists with field experience, or for those with understanding of waste remediation.

PLANNING FOR THE FUTURE

The information in this book is only meant to be an introduction to environmental science and to some of the career opportunities available in environmental science and related fields. If you think you are interested in a career in environmental science, it is never too early to start learning your options or to begin gaining experience.

- Speak to a school guidance counselor to get advice on how to find student job opportunities in your area.

- A science teacher, or local environmental scientist may be able to **mentor** you or offer additional instruction in proper equipment use or laboratory procedure.

Choosing a career in environmental science will be fulfilling for you and may help protect the future of the entire planet.

- Learn about local organizations that are active in environmental protection and preservation. You may be able to volunteer to help with some of their projects.

- Participate in—or start—an environmental group at your school. Perhaps you can devise ways to make your school (or even your town) greener.

Everything you do that is related to your interest in environmental science will help guide you to the specialization for which you are most suited and will strengthen you in the eyes of *prospective* schools or employers.

If You Have an Artistic Personality . . .

Environmental science may not be the right career choice for you, as it will not offer you as many opportunities for self-expression and creativity.

If You Have a Conventional Personality . . .

Here are some of the best jobs for you in environmental science.

JOB	ANNUAL EARNINGS	ANNUAL OPENINGS
inspectors, testers, samplers	$33,640	8,300
environmental science & protection technician	$39,370	8,400

FURTHER READING

Arms, Karen. *Environmental Science*. Geneva, Ill.: Holt McDougal, 2007.

Camenson, Blythe. *Great Jobs for Geology Majors*. Chicago, Ill.: VGM Career Horizons, 2000.

Cassio, Jim and Alice Rush. *Green Careers: Choosing Work for a Sustainable Future*. Gabriola Island, B.C., Canada: New Society Publishers, 2009.

Deitche, Scott M. *Green Collar Jobs: Environmental Careers for the 21st Century*. Santa Barbara, Calif.: Praeger, 2010.

Lore, Nicholas. *Now What?: The Young Person's Guide to Choosing the Perfect Career*. New York: Fireside, 2008.

Wheeler, Benjamin, Gilda Wheeler and Wendy Church. *It's All Connected: A Comprehensive Guide to Global Issues and Sustainable Solutions*. Seattle, Wash.: Facing the Future, 2005.

Wright, Richard T. *Environmental Science: Toward a Sustainable Future*. Upper Saddle River, N.J.: Prentice Hall, 2007.

FIND OUT MORE ON THE INTERNET

Career Compass
www.careervoyages.gov/careercompass-main.cfm

Environmental Protection Agency
Career Opportunities for Students
www.epa.gov/ohr/careers/stuopp.html#hs

Green Careers Center
www.environmentalcareer.com

National Oceanic and Atmospheric Administration (NOAA)
www.noaa.gov

United States Department of Agriculture (USDA)
Natural Resources and Environment
www.usda.gov/wps/portal/!ut/p/_s.7_0_A/7_0_1OB?navtype=SU&n
avid=NATURAL_RESOURCES

USA Jobs
Student Jobs
www.usajobs.gov/studentjobs/

USGS
Apply for Student Jobs
www.usgs.gov/ohr/student/apply/index.html

DISCLAIMER

The websites listed on this page were active at the time of publication. The publisher is not responsible for websites that have changed their address or discontinued operation since the date of publication. The publisher will review and update the websites upon each reprint.

BIBLIOGRAPHY

Making the Difference. "Environmental Science Jobs in the Federal Government," makingthedifference.org/federalcareers/environmental.shtml (19 February 2010).

National Oceanic and Atmospheric Administration. "Paleoclimatology," www.ncdc.noaa.gov/paleo/paleo.html (8 March 2010).

Ramey, Alice. "Going "Green": Environmental Jobs for Scientists and Engineers." *Occupational Outlook Quarterly*, Summer 2009.

United Nations Population Division. "World Population Trends," www.un.org/popin/wdtrends.htm (7 March 2010).

United States Department of Labor, Bureau of Labor Statistics. "Environmental Scientists and Specialists," www.bls.gov/oco/ocos311.htm (16 February 2010).

United States Department of Labor, Bureau of Labor Statistics. "Geosientists and Hydrologists," www.bls.gov/oco/ocos312.htm (16 February 2010).

United States Department of Labor, Bureau of Labor Statistics. "Science Technicians," www.bls.gov/oco/ocos115.htm (16 February 2010).

United States Environmental Protection Agency (EPA). "Air," www.epa.gov/ebtpages/air.html (26 February 2010).

United States Environmental Protection Agency (EPA). "Learn the Issues," www.epa.gov/epahome/learn.htm (25 February 2010).

United States Environmental Protection Agency (EPA). "Water Pollution," www.epa.gov/ebtpages/watewaterpollution.html (26 February 2010).

United States Geological Survey (USGS). "Water Science for Schools," http://ga.water.usgs.gov/edu/ (26 February 2010).

Utah Department of Natural Resources. "Loving Our Jobs," naturalresources.utah.gov/employment/love-their-jobs/environmental-scientist.html (25 February 2010).

INDEX

PICTURE CREDITS

Fotolia: pg 8
    Alex Bramwell: pg. 8
    amelie: pg. 32

cubephoto: pg. 20
Galyna Andrushko: pg. 52
Rick Carlson: pg. 42

To the best knowledge of the publisher, all images not specifically credited are in the public domain. If any image has been inadvertently uncredited, please notify Harding House Publishing Service, 220 Front Street, Vestal, New York 13850, so that credit can be given in future printings.

ABOUT THE AUTHOR

Cordelia Strange has a master's degree from Binghamton University and is especially interested in health, the environment, and education. She enjoys applying these interests (and others) in writing books for young people.

ABOUT THE CONSULTANT

Michael Puglisi is the director of the Department of Labor's Workforce New York One Stop Center in Binghamton, New York. He has also held several leadership positions in the International Association of Workforce Professionals (IAWP), a non-profit educational association exclusively dedicated to workforce professionals with a rich tradition and history of contributions to workforce excellence. IAWP members receive the tools and resources they need to effectively contribute to the workforce development system daily. By providing relevant education, timely and informative communication and valuable findings of pertinent research, IAWP equips its members with knowledge, information and practical tools for success. Through its network of local and regional chapters, IAWP is preparing its members for the challenges of tomorrow.